"Dancing with Daddy's Memory"

Once upon a time in a cozy little town, there lived a sweet little girl named Nariyah. When Nariyah was only three years old, her father, Raphael, a happy, bubbly spirit who adored reggae music and dancing, passed away unexpectedly. Since then, Nariyah lived with her loving mother, who did her best to fill their home with warmth and love.

Now at the age of seven, Nariyah sometimes felt a twinge of sadness in her heart when she thought about her dad not being there with her.

But she found comfort in the memories shared, especially those captured in videos on her mother's phone. Among them were precious moments of her dad dancing with her in his arms, swaying to the rhythm of their favorite reggae tunes.

Nariyah often reminisced about the times she and her dad would sit and eat cornmeal porridge that her grandma used to make, a simple joy that always brought a smile to her face.

Whenever Nariyah missed her dad, she would snuggle up with her favorite teddy bear, a soft and cuddly companion who listened patiently as she poured out her feelings. She would tell her teddy about her day, share memories of her dad, and sometimes even dance around the room, pretending her dad was right there with her.

One sunny afternoon, as Nariyah watched one of the videos of her dad dancing, she felt a wave of happiness wash over her.

She could almost feel her dad's presence, his laughter filling the room

as they twirled around together. Inspired by the joyful memories,

Nariyah decided to honor her dad's love for dancing in a special way.

With her teddy bear as her dance partner, Nariyah put on her favorite reggae song and started moving to the beat. As she danced, she imagined her dad watching from above, smiling proudly at his little girl. In that moment, Nariyah felt a sense of peace and connection that filled her heart with warmth.

From that day on, whenever Nariyah felt sad or lonely, she knew she could always turn to her memories and her teddy bear for comfort.

And as she danced and laughed, she felt her dad's love surrounding her, reminding her that he would always be a part of her life, guiding her with his love from afar.

Printed in Great Britain
by Amazon